Blue Hour

Blue Hour
Jo McNeice

Winner of the
Kathleen Grattan
Poetry Award

OTAGO UNIVERSITY PRESS
Te Whare Tā o Ōtākou Whakaihu Waka

For Bella

CONTENTS

- 7   Aro Valley
- 8   This summer
- 9   An analysis of us as a film
- 16   I've said too much
- 17   Wolf
- 19   Mermaid singing (i)
- 21   Tidal
- 23   Laura
- 25   Guilt
- 26   Not out of the woods yet
- 28   Compartment C
- 30   Candles squint into the sun
- 31   Schizoaffective in spring
- 34   Angels
- 35   Spring
- 36   Another of my bloody love poems
- 37   Ghostheart
- 38   Mermaid singing (ii)
- 41   Bees haunt the sunflowers
- 42   You & me
- 44   She's feeling old
- 48   Maybe
- 51   Kiss
- 52   Flicker
- 53   Going where I have to go

55	Night falls fast
56	Admission
58	Purgatory
60	Love song, 1990s
61	Although I have never met you, you have shipwrecked my heart
62	Mermaid singing (iii)
63	The exam of shedding light
64	Apology
65	Blue hour
66	*Notes*
67	*Acknowledgements*

Aro Valley

I want to take
your picture.
The silver blue
mist moving
over the pine trees,
the Edwardian houses
running backwards
up the hillside,
the road running
slower than myself.
The sky a kind of
silver screen,
the moon is out tonight.
A neon TV.
A noticeboard.
The buttery light
melting out of the chip shop
into the indigo air.
The weeds tripping up
the fences, the flowers
tripping up the weeds.
The night about to settle
in for the night.
But pausing before
it closes the door.
Relax. I think you look
just wonderful.
I imagine you can tell
I want to take your picture.

This summer

What you notice most about
this summer
are the dandelions.

There are dandelions
everywhere
outside the dental clinic,
lining the hills
of the Aro Valley
with tiny yellow bricks.

Millions of stars
in the emerald sky.

An analysis of us as a film

Light & dark,
deception & betrayal
(wait, that's not us).

We are an undiscovered language.
If we are not careful, we will be extinct
before the linguists find us,
before we find each other.

There's a hero
his brown paper bag holding a bottle of gin –
but we're not there yet.

Ordinary world,
conflict,
change,
failure.
Comment on the mythical,
goals ambiguous,
deconstructed genres.

There's someone,
a mother figure, always
reading over my shoulder.

Don't worry,
I am very careful
to write you in anonymously,
like the ghost who lives in the TV.

Although it's only me
who is worried about the fallout.

No one can believe
the hero's metamorphosis
from drunken loser
with multiple delusions,
sadness running down his
arms in dark red beads,
to the guy who scrubs up well,
holds down a steady job,
hasn't been to the emergency
department in nearly a year.

You know he's chatting with his
psychiatrist about you.
Asking him 'What to do? What to do?'
It's a long shot that anything will happen.

Like I said before,
we are a language,
we may be critically endangered.

But there are obstacles to overcome:
a domineering mother,
an uptight establishment,
a meandering narrative,
more than one antagonist.
A swarm of killer bees &
a psychopath waiting in the woods.

There's a city street after dark
in summer where old men are
playing dominoes.

There's a tracking shot down
an alley, a cat runs through
a hole in the fence. There's
a body falling from the sky.

After a close-up of your face
the hero's buddy tells him
'You're fucking overweight,
it's never going to happen
with someone so attractive.'
The hero is sick of being told shit
like this over & over by his so-called buddy.

Outside we know it's spring
by the way the gorse is blooming

by the way the celluloid
captures the darkness of the pine trees,
the gentle curve of the horse's neck
echoed in the curve of the stream.

The hero is about to crack.
He walks past liquor stores
but is afraid to go in, in case
mother is watching
from the car she's followed him in.

His hands shake, his heart is a
greyhound chasing a rabbit.
Instead he throws back lorazepam &
vows to take ice baths to cure himself
of this affliction.

His buddy tells him
'Let it die, let it die, there's nothing there.
Besides, everyone knows fat is unattractive.'

We have our own particular syntax,
our own accent.
Please bring an auxiliary verb:
must, shall, will.
Necessity or possibility.

Lying in the basement bedroom
of his parents' house, curtains
drawn against the light
the hero hears his buddy's voice:

'Get a grip, get a grip. Anyway,
studies show that ninety percent
of people are turned off by excess body weight.
It would be especially true
given the body in this case.'

He starts to imagine a fiery car wreck
somewhere in Act Three
after a long chase.

He gets up & goes into the kitchen
the walls are the colour of
rancid butter. Mother waits
to serve him tea.

Central characters are often anti-heroes,
failures & losers.
Characters lack goals, therefore
narratives are not structured by
logic of causality.
Tighter framing, faster cutting.

'I'm only looking out for you,'
the hero's buddy tells him.

You know, we are irregular verbs.
You know the universe is harsh.

Yet there must be a scene where
a train travels through the desert,
mustangs grazing
among desert flowers.

The hero wears a Stetson as he
writes this scene:
people are drinking in the dining car,
there are footsteps on the roof
coming closer, shots are fired & then –

But still mother is watching
him in the background. She is the damp
spot on the ceiling.
Holding a cup of tea in one hand,
 a rosary in the other.

Some fast cut sequences remain
spatially coherent. Increased use
of wide-angle lenses.
Exaggerated distance between
background & foreground.
Shadows fragment the frame.

He hears the voiceover of his friend:
'I am alone. You should be too.'

Together we translate a sentence.
The evenings are lengthening.

Silver trees against silver sky.
A sliver of light under the door.

The hero can't eat when he knows
he is about to see you.
Lovesick & weak
he takes up jogging.

Pessimism & anxiety.
Nightmarish qualities.
Audience insecurity.
Fate is key.

He counts down the days
until he sees you but
his friend tells him
'You're wasting your time.
You're not good enough.
I'm doing you a favour.'

Unhappy endings.
Flashbacks complex.
Tracks & pans interrupted by cuts.
Free ranging camera movement.

He wants to say
'Would you like to go for coffee?'
He practises daily.
He looks at his hands.

I've said too much

You were there trying to kiss
me with a mouth full of food.

I was wearing a dressing gown,
planting hellebores,

running away from paramedics,
pulling out an IV line.

& you were taking me apart
with your teeth, so white.

As the moon watched from above,
I was gardening in the dark.

Scattering mustard seed
& lurking like a bumble bee

around a borage flower.
Watching like the kingfisher

waiting for the newt to rise.
You were the ladybird

flying back to your burning
house.

I think I set
this fire myself.

Wolf

There's a train, old hero, grey beard of steam
flickering on the screen,   running down the line.
In the distance of the late afternoon,
                                   cup of tea in my hand,
 I see a white owl fly low over a field.
 In the deception of the evening
                             a badger walks out of the woods
into the path of an oncoming car.
A man & his dog find a deer in the woods
                                  & bang she's gone.
You never do that, a woman tells her daughter-in-law
                                      over & over again.
In the yellow kitchen of a dark wood house,
                                the girl finds lead shot in her teeth.
The man's mouth produces saliva, forming words
he will not speak.
Instead he turns to me & asks
              why are you here? What is your purpose here?
I shut my mouth.   Swallow back my fear.
It is something from a French horror film.
I recognise it.
There's a woman with a small dog, searching in a hollow for a lamb.
She finds herself in a quagmire,
skirt muddy, pulling herself up.
The dog, the lamb & I run.
She grabs at leaves & roots, is dragged down
                           into the mud, beast on her back.
Her fear embeds itself under my nails,
black, tasting of the countryside.

Wouldn't he love to chew her up, wouldn't he love to –
              these things
that mushroom
       in the kitchen, in the dining room.
In the deceiving evening light, there's a train, some miles away.
       I run towards it.

Mermaid singing (i)

The mermaid
braided her hair.

Red, it reached
down her back.

Lying on a rock
she sang:

Why do you write in my notes
that I take cocaine?
I have never taken cocaine.
Why do you wear parachute pants
with white sneakers?
It's not 1983.

The mermaid peeled back
her fish tail.

She found a foot.
Then another.

Painted her toenails
red
just as some
old women do.

She called up her mum
& told her

'I will never willingly
take the medication again,
they will have to inject me.
Hold me down & inject me.'

Her mum said
'That won't happen again.'

The tide came in.
The tide went out.

The psychiatrist asked
'Will you take this?
Good girl.'

A gang of seagulls stalked
a crab down the beach
leaving only an empty shell.

The mermaid sang:

Am I a monkey & a fish
stitched together –
a P.T. Barnum hoax?
Are my tears really pearls
or is this just sand in my eye?

One night as the nurses held her
down & injected her she sang:

Where are my fins disappearing to?
& why don't I have wings?

Tidal

Through a fisheye lens
through & through.

The psychiatrist says
'It's your life.'

White lights shine out of paper,
blue lights in the air.

Yellow lights appear
on people's heads.

Drops of blood
on my hands –

ants through desert sand.
Angels like carrier pigeons

darken the sky.
A postcard came this morning
soaking wet:

Resolution in the sea.
Cherry tree. Fish eggs,
dulse & carrageenan.
Silver tongues, catching tiny fish.
Messages delivered through
serrated teeth.
Now just you wait

*with your mermaid scales
desiccating. Buried in
the sand. Eyes open,
waves washing over
the top of you.*

All this life blooming
in the water.
All this life blooming
in water.

Laura

A glosa after 'The Age of Gold' by P.K. Page.

A flock of pigeons splayed
themselves against the sky,
your absence greater the next day.
I went to bed with a migraine,
the psychiatrist (of all people)
said to me 'you poor girl,
maybe it was psychic pain.'
I cursed myself for not waving
at that bloody magpie.
Day followed night, the sky

never standing still.
A blackbird in the leaves
through the window
as dawn stretched its legs
across the hills.
You had discussed the way
you were going to die,
I took no notice, thought you
were demented. The day was
cloudless, the air sweet-scented.

Sparrows dropped from a plum tree,
nestled in the dirt below.
Grass bowed down in the wind & rain
it all went on, all the same.
I think of your father,

head bowed, trying not to cry.
I think of your mother,
brittle, trying not to cry.
Morose thoughts alone in bars,
night followed day, the stars

all awake in the darkening sky.
Birds tucked their heads under wing.
Your voice in the song of a bird?
I don't think so.
Your soul in the body of a bird?
I don't know.
Your mother said you're in the sky
looking down on us.
All this time, the stars abiding,
bright – Orion striding.

Guilt

The unwelcome visitor
who brings a plate of baking,
the recipe is your own.

Not out of the woods yet

In this glade
where I find the cottage
I find myself breaking
gingerbread tiles from the roof,
nibbling on a candy cane bannister,
face pressed up to the window
licking glass made of melted sugar.
Trying to keep the wolf
who lives within, out.
Trying to keep her from the door.

Yes, I was a beast once.
Truthfully, it was many times more.
Mixed my metaphors
with too much gin, in a teacup decorated
with burgundy roses & gold trim
& now as I follow
a trail of crumbs through the forest
shadows falling, shadows stumbling,
I pull up my red hood,
& quicken my step.

Bristles sprouting on my chin,
I think I could feign
being Grandmama.
Dressing up appeals
& the thought
of the axe making a seam
down my belly

& a calloused hand pulling out
the people I've consumed.

Still a creature waits in a crooked little house.
She dresses all in black, as if each day
there is a funeral to attend.
She milks the cows for her cats,
lights the oven, kneads bread.

I tell myself not to be afraid.
I will myself, *don't be afraid.*
It's not easy. She knows
I have the dirt on her.
It's been collecting under
my fingernails like fliers in
the letterbox of an empty house.

Compartment C

The air was spring.
The ground was winter.
She travelled through the seasons
like a bar-tailed godwit.
The green interior of the compartment
remembered each traveller.
The green faded like a patchwork
of hills against a purple sky.

Thunder without rain.
A drop   a fall.
A smudge
of trees against reddening earth.
A smudge   of thoughts
in the desert, in the desert.

She looked up.
A downpour   of thought:
The piano drowns at midnight
in a sea of yellow tigers.
Bring me a cup of tea.
No, thank you.
Just the blood from the cactus thumb.

In the desert
a murmur of green.
Her mind desert then forest.
Desert/forest,
desert/forest.

Drought & deluge,

deluge & drought.

The sky fed her thoughts.

Her mind the compartment,
stillness & motion.
Thoughts at once
 terrifying & mysterious.
The green remembered her.

Candles squint into the sun

By old Saint Paul's
bodies lie on the cobblestones,
their limbs at odd angles.
There's a woman in beige tights
& black shoes.
A policeman waits, chalk in pocket.
Across the street a crowd gathers.
I walk the narrow road
between them
tiptoeing to avoid
the blood spatter
on the pavement.

A blackbird flies onto my hand.
I feed it crumbs
I found on the trail.
Death makes his way
down the path beside me,
humming a sweet &
salty tune.
The blackbird tips
his hat, flies away.

Schizoaffective in spring

They are just hedging
their bets, these skeletons
dressed in skin, & false
promises
who look into your head
with nothing but the cavities
where eyes should sit.

First they tell you you are
the wasted stamp on a
dead letter, the flick of ash
from a menthol cigarette,
the semen that dripped
through the slats
of the gallows.

Then they say you are
the rattle of matches, a
stingray's barb,
the air under the canopy
of the parachute.

They pound you
until they are done,
roll off then
kiss you passionately

call you later
to deliver

the sucker punch,
kiss you again
on your bloodied mouth,
long black tongues
reaching you
down the line.

But

the fact —

it remains
everybody & no one knows it
it's not a buck each way,
a roll of the dice.
It's not a friendly Labrador
or your four-leaf clover.

You are just
molecules erasing
themselves,
a collection of
moments & dust,
a melted bullet,
an empty cartridge,
the point at which
the day starts
turning.

& everybody knows
that you are just
phoning it in

until that hour
it all gives way

until your bones
start burning.

Angels

I could see them nowhere.
To add to the mystery
do not mention
what you feel,
that you see
the real me
up on the ceiling,
separate & dead.
I looked down by chance.
What they do is nothing
to do with me.

Spring

It seems so familiar, as if I am repeating
a play to an audience that seldom changes.
Outside, a blustery wind, the rain just keeps on falling.
Whispered asides from the wings. I'm flailing,
my costume is missing a button, the sleeve is torn.
It's as if I am repeating
the same old story to someone who plainly is not listening.
On stage I'm unravelling my sins, channelling your pain.
Outside, a blustery wind, the rain just keeps on falling.
The playbills keep piling up, I'm drowning.
Swim to me, reach out your hand – I'll pull you down.
It all seems so familiar as if I am repeating
my thoughts on the circularity of time.
All these blown lightbulbs in the dressing room.
The ceiling's a heartbeat, it grows, then closes in.
From the cheap seats, a stifled cough, tired sighs.
It all seems so familiar, as if I am repeating myself.
Outside, a blustery wind, the rain just keeps on falling.

Another of my bloody love poems

It's an old dog
of an idea.
Deaf, incontinent
& milky-eyed.

I found her
on a path in the suburbs,
walking in circles,
stumbling.
I stood there awhile
wondering what to do.
Was there anything to do?

Then a voice.
'That's Prudence,
she's out for her walk.'
A woman with a platinum
blonde bob appeared
from a character home.

Relieved, it wasn't my problem,
& a little ill.
How can something
in such a state
be kept alive?

Ghostheart

You strip the muscle with detergent,
then you say 'I treated you badly'.
You say it three times, like a spell,
like you want absolution,
like magical thinking works.
These things happen.

Structural integrity remains –
scaffolding a desert shade of white.
Structure is crucial, the darkness of night.
You tell me it's because I have bipolar disorder.
A ventricle, an atrium stripped of origin,
life & its particulars, obliterated.
I try to bilocate.

The rain will fall, the sky will not.
Immature cells can be programmed.
You ask me when my birthday is.
(You never asked before now.)
Grow up.
You are creating a personalised heart,
which you can grind up,
make a powder, make a gel.
Design & create, chase your goal
till all that remains
remains:
a flicker of pulse,
               a tiny beat of heart.

Mermaid singing (ii)

The mermaid, comb in her hand,
lay on her rock & sang:

he's jumping my bones

he's sucking out the marrow
using the bed sheet as a serviette.

Maybe when he's done with my bones
he'll feed them to his dog
(who likes to fish for stones).

Bones made up of crystals
shaped like hands & fingers.
He held my hand & told me
I was the ocean.
He should know,
he used to dive.

The mermaid looked in her mirror,
heard a human voice.
'Mermaids are sometimes
monstrously ugly.'

She began to sing:

Sometimes I think
of drowning & I see
this shark with a mechanical smile

*so wide
that it touches the sides
of who knows where.
Would my hand wave?
I can't see why.*

*Don't hold your breath
on the dive, or you will end up paralysed.
Well, it's more of a fall really,
& it's clear I'm falling.*

*& now
I dislocate & break.*

*If I wake up
with sand in my ear*

will he still introduce himself?

*Let's discuss the advantages
of life in open water.*

(If I wake up.)

*& I lose a little
of what I've gained
50 fathoms deep.*

Coming up,

*I do not appear to have inhaled
salt water.*

*I do not appear to be
a bludgeoned seal.*

*& in his quiet moments
does he ask himself if he succeeded?
Or does he just ponder the way a ladybird
sees the world or why there's an explosion
of jellyfish on the coast this year.*

She sings:

*All I know is that the tide is coming in,
& there's a westerly wind.*

Bees haunt the sunflowers

Bees haunt the sunflowers, ghosts with places to go.
I am not everything you think I am, or what you say.
These fallacies you sell me, they'll disappear in the afterglow.

These lies you tell, they rise & fall, get swallowed by the undertow.
Still, you spoon-feed them to me in every way.
Bees haunt the sunflowers, ghosts with places to go.

You plough me, fuck me, let go on me, you jump my bones.
You are a small tornado. Trees like me, we bow & scrape.
These fallacies you sell me, they'll disappear in the afterglow.

Weeds sprout up, allegro, smother the vege patch; the lawn's unmown,
the garden waits, the soil is clay.
Bees haunt the sunflowers, ghosts with places to go.

Sunflower pollen is medicine for bumble bees, I didn't know!
All this time, this repetition, don't you think that it gets stale?
These fallacies you sell me, they'll disappear in the afterglow.

The winged insects are free to fly, off they go.
It's a reflex. I am paralysed. Still I pray.
Bees haunt the sunflowers, ghosts with places to go.
These fallacies you sell me, they'll disappear in the afterglow.

You & me

*A glosa after 'Calmly We Walk through This April's day'
by Delmore Schwartz.*

I stand on the edge of autumn
on the verge of the afternoon.
All my bad decisions have followed me home.
They watch the house from
across the street, casually
smoking cigarettes & flicking ash.
Is it menace or concern?
From this distance it's hard to tell.
Do they see what you see?
What will become of you and me?

Sounds roam your house & pack
themselves into a tired suitcase.
My body sags under the weight of your
indifference, the weight of your distraction,
the load of your obsession.
I start to speak, you finish,
although I would like to point out
it's wind turbines, not windmills.
Never mind, take your turn.
(This is the school in which we learn.)

There's an upstairs room with a bed
made up for me, that I've never seen.
We wash your sheets, get rid
of the smell of us.

I tell myself I don't exist, that
everything gets swept away,
not even my bitterness remains.
Like the bridge on our riverside picnic,
eventually almost everything gets washed away.
Besides the photo and the memory.

My poor choices are knocking
at the door, like your nosy neighbour
standing on the step, waiting for you to answer.
We pretend there's no one home.
Did they hear us? The windows were open.
We lie in your bed, guess the hour. It's way past
noon in late summer or maybe
autumn, turns out to you it's all the same.
I don't know yet that I won't return, or
that time is the fire in which we burn.

She's feeling old

Forget the deliciousness of clouds,
salt water,

barren moonscapes on earth,
falling morning light,

the window of a chapel.
Forget it all.

At the bay, I'm curled
on the sand. I'm an ampersand

& my heart is a utilitarian
1950s tower block of council flats.

The need to demolish ugliness
lives within most of us,

to rid ourselves & our surroundings
of unpleasantness, or what we think is

ugly. Distasteful. Hideous.
At heart we can all be brutal.

My council flat heart is inhabited by life
in a state of decay. Disorder. Disintegration.

Disobeying. Is there anything sadder
than a man pissing

in the stairwell of
his own home?

Of course there is, there are many,
many things:

in a drought, clouds that
suggest rain, but come to nothing,

a tethered dog with an
empty water bowl,

a Jurassic lothario trawling
the internet for 19-year-olds.

I try writing to a lover
who doesn't understand

Modernist architecture,
who prefers the hearts he keeps

lusting after to be Gothic or mediaeval,
a church or cathedral

that would never,
be considered for demolition.

A place visitors flock to,
to have a reverential experience

regardless of faith.
He lights a candle, says a prayer.

The tower block is not, &
never was, they say, fit for purpose.

He laments its ugliness, a rough
blandness that irritates him.

At the bay, on the sand
curled up like an ampersand,

I wish my heart was
the Italian chapel on Orkney.

Two Nissan huts joined together,
corrugated interior covered with

concrete, something beautiful made
out of not very much,

peace being constructed
by prisoners of war,

light-holders made of corned beef tins,
baptismal font from a car exhaust,

tabernacle crafted out of
wood from a shipwreck,

a tiny metal heart in the
floor under the gates, an echo.

The tower block heart
knows what is coming.

& yet it once had pot plants
on window sills,

sofas covered with crocheted blankets,
framed pictures of family.

Dinners cooking on the stove, a half-finished
crossword, *Women's Weekly* on the coffee table.

A tower block heart knows its pain is very ordinary,
very plain, basic, ugly even. Forgettable.

Some types of pain are just more
pleasing to the eye. Now

my lover takes the driver's seat in the
crane that swings the wrecking ball.

Maybe

it has happened
smoke & sirens
sparks & ash.

I don't know yet
how much I will come to
loathe myself, even if
you lie to me &
tell me I am beautiful.

Maybe I will
compare myself to mythical &
historical figures, something bullshit
& grandiose like that,
even though this is more like
an episode of Peep Show.

I think of the myth
behind the name
Heliotrope which I have
growing in the garden.
It reminds me of us.
Of course it does, everything does,
even though there is no us & there never was.

I am Clytes, purple with despair,
you are Helios
'in love' with someone else,
'in love' with anyone except me.

I will write about it, give everyone
vaguely disguised names or
something as equally fucking stupid as that.
I will go to the beach & weep
I will starve myself
(but only for a couple of days)
or something overwrought like that.

I will be bitter, bitter – go on, taste it.
Still I will deliver myself to you,
like a piece of low-hanging fruit,
even though I know there's nowhere
in this to go.
Even though you wear – well,
we all make certain choices.

But maybe

I will channel Joan of Arc today,
hand back your nettle & gorse bouquet.
I will wear an armour made
of my misery & mania,
delusions & hallucinations,
fight my way out of this.

All this way away from you.
All this way to get so far from you.

Maybe I will tell you

*You thought to deceive me
but it is yourself you deceive,*

deprive you of the redemption arc
you seem to be so desperately seeking.

Maybe I will
commando crawl out of
this dumpster fire we created.

Maybe I will
watch it

burn

Kiss

How much does it mean to me, to you?
It's the end of the message, a tiny spark flying through dark.

It's the rabbit sitting upright in the grass, or the one
you pull from your hat, a spell to undo dark.

It's the crumb in front of me, a sweet nothing
on the forest floor wandering a path through dark.

It marks your spot, leave it out now, you hope
I will fade away. Endings without it lead into dark.

It's the gristle to choke on, a slab of insincerity that can't
be swallowed, now even light can't break through dark.

It can be the noise of steel on steel or
a calculated ending, from a heart that's just sinew. dark.

I am devastated by my own curiosity
you thought you'd keep me in this dreaded blue dark.

I've found a key to open the door, didn't realise you
were behind me. Waiting to lock me in a brand-new dark.

Flicker

I dig myself a hole
with the spade you hand to me.
In the backyard behind your
Hansel & Gretel house,
hens pecking in the dirt,
passion fruit vine throttling the lime,
sweat runs down my forehead,
a wasp crawls over a plank of wood.
So plump – it's a queen, you & I agree.
You take off your jandal, the job is done.
I turn to you & smile adoringly.
The hole is nearly ready.
Who has come before, who will come after?
But there's a flicker beyond the dull light
somewhere. It will begin again.

Going where I have to go

A glosa after 'The Waking' by Theodore Roethke.

There I go again, driving past fields of cows.
They know who & what I am – spindles of fear.
But maybe I mistake me for myself,
maybe I let go too soon.
Rain treads softly on the roof,
the night is finely divided & open.
Sugar these pills, give the dog a bone.
Rain treads heavily outside the window.
Wandering through city streets filled with cattle,
I wake to sleep, and take my waking slow.

My eyes are black. Nothing is what it seems.
There's only itchy noise from the 1940s radio.
I climb into your bed – it collapses.
Each time I come back to life
the mirror lies then tells the truth.
The TV is on in an empty house,
clouds come rolling in, I come rolling home.
Another woman's hair clip on your bedside table.
Why am I here? You rebuild a bed of nails.
I feel my fate in what I cannot fear.

In an empty movie theatre
Robert Mitchum casts his spell.
I'm on my knees, praying to Mary,
messing around, looking for keys.
It dawns on me what's being created.

My head is being knick-knacked.
Voices, dark blue, slip in & out
corrupting what I really know.
I've looked skyward so long colours start to run.
I learn by going where I have to go.

My heart diseases my body, my mind.
It crackles like static on the screen.
2:49 a.m.: the downpour becomes a deluge.
Maybe I'd forgotten or didn't want to hear
we change the landscape we walk through
movie-like, time after time.
I wake a little older, soft-bodied, without a glow.
Outside, dawn breaks cleanly & just so.
Can't stop what's coming, what's already here.
We think by feeling. What is there to know?

Night falls fast

I thought I saw your
shadow on the stairs,
first behind me
then ahead.
The house was silent,
a pond frozen over.
I remembered a book
you'd given me,
one I shouldn't have read.
Your reflection as I passed
the mirror in the hall upstairs?
Because for a moment it wasn't mine.
I went forward, made a fingerprint
on the glass. But it was a trick
of the light, made by the shadows
of the fast falling night.

Admission

Admit nothing.
Your mind is a blizzard.
All the eyes of the creatures
from the bottom of the ocean
are on you.
You have planted rue & honesty
in a patch of salty black earth,
ingested doubt, like
a daily dose of arsenic.

There's a man who lives near Pork Chop Hill.
He does not even like you & never will.
He has fed you kerbside blackberries,
shown you how the fleabane grows.
He's had you, but he doesn't get you
& that's the way it goes.

May the cat eat you & the devil
eat the cat.
Nature is ill, but she won't admit it.
You have come face-to-face
with a stone fish,
clutched at the pearls around
your neck standing at the bus stop
through winters of sleet & snow.
You have heard the scream
of the mandrake
being pulled from the earth.
You have drunk the sap

of the hellebore –
poison is the only cure for madness because
poison is the only cure for madness.

Purgatory

Maybe it's misfortune,
maybe it's your own design
or some corruption in between.
Witnesses click their tongues,
mouths like chests of treasure.
There's a lesion in your reckoning.

It is easy to believe in the rain,
pale & sweet that keeps on falling,
for centuries.
What do you find in your hand?
Consider it nothing more than an atlas
mapping out your indifference, ingratitude, presumption.
Consider it as useful as the compass
with a bent needle.
By & by the rain turns the ground to mud.

It is the off-key note as you sing your way
through the cemetery.
Cherubs coyly lifting the corners of their dresses.
Statues with pretty, no, beautiful faces
half-knocked off, missing a limb or two.
Angels whose throats bleed from an eternity
of singing.
Rabbits getting it on.

The maze of errors you
have constructed around yourself
in this terrain is extensive.

Consider the misfortune
of others at your hand.
You know the bed, it's not yours
but it is familiar.
It's made, it's unmade.
There is a sign at night.
The sky glistens with your
mistakes.

Love song, 1990s

I don't know why you wait for me.
Moments are bound then released.
There are crows that become commas
in the trees & dashes in the sky.
One for sorrow, I can't say why.

You'd like to tell me what you think
I've come here looking for.
There's a smell of smoke in the air.
Somewhere, someone is poring over
a photograph album, snapshots of
people, faces not unlike our own.
Not far from here a memory unearthed,
a recollection in waking sleep.

I am waiting for the snow
to see two lambs carved in stone.
I try to read the signs that
I know are meant for me.
A billboard, postcard, dog
on a leash, an oak leaf.

A fox runs through the garden
the camera is set up on the lawn
& here within our confines we meet.

You hold out your hand to me.
Am I a familiar face
or just a leaf that's falling?

Although I have never met you, you have
shipwrecked my heart

I thought it was me who had the upper hand,

    stealing souls, cursing sailors, fixated on my mirror,

        my heart the Flying Dutchman, my heart a rabbit's foot,
        my heart a potato, roughly peeled.

& the weather – clouds like the darkest delphinium petals on the horizon,

    a southerly that came racing in, like a manic episode.

You extended your hand to me, you didn't know I was drowning in air

    or that angels really were listening to your thoughts.

In the empty moments, the night webbed with stars,

    I doubted your existence, like I began to doubt my own.

I held up the obedient mirror, tilted it to find the light.

    Saw a collision of treasure chests, sea foam,
    sharks' teeth & gills
        drowning sailors
            burning masts, desperation & desire.

Mermaid singing (iii)

We are the rain, the thunder
& we are on fire, my dear
& we are on fire.

The sky is an adamant shade of green.
Stars are collapsing inwards.
The birds unhook their wings from the air.

& we burn in this dark weather
& we drown in this dead weather.

The exam of shedding light

is beginning. You have no words,
no answers, nothing to say,
to write on this page that grows
& shrinks before your eyes.

There are only images:
the lobby of a derelict hotel,
a house half-filled with sand,
moss & ferns growing inside a collapsing villa,
roller coaster carriages in an abandoned theme park,
an empty jacuzzi in a forgotten swingers' club.

You drum your fingers on the desk,
chew the end of your HB pencil –
the lead has fallen out.
It's you & you & you again,
alone here with all the noise
of the empty auditorium.

Apology

I dreamt of you,
alive.
Yellow corridors &
rain for days.
An office?
A house in the suburbs
with a storm about to descend?
I can't recall.
A photo that didn't come out right,
the negative disturbed.
I dreamt of you.

Blue hour

Meet me in the photograph
somewhere in colour.
Now is twilight – lemon
seeping into violet.
The orange windows of houses
match the orange horizon,
inky night sliding in.
Where lust is bleeding
into longing, violet
turns to indigo.
In black & white
we appear to glow.
Meet me on the silver gelatin
(a sliver of death preserving life).
Meet me in the in-between
where the negative
is being developed.
Let us capture something
before the impenetrable
blackness.

Notes

'An analysis of us as a film' contains found elements from lecture notes from a Victoria University of Wellington Film Studies paper FILM 234, 2009, which draws on the work of David Bordwell.

'Laura' is a glosa that uses lines with variation from 'The Age of Gold' by P.K. Page.

'Angels' is a found poem, using phrases from *Schizophrenia: A very short introduction* by Christopher, D. Frith (Oxford: Oxford University Press, 2003).

'Ghostheart' was inspired by an article about ghost hearts – pigs' hearts that have been cleaned, leaving white scaffolding that is injected with a patient's cells.

'You & me' is a glosa that uses lines with variation from from 'Calmly We Walk through This April's day' by Delmore Schwartz.

'Maybe': *You thought to deceive me / but it is yourself you deceive* is a quote from *Joan of Arc: In her own words* (New York: Books & Co, 1996).

'Going where I have to go' is a glosa using lines from 'The Waking' by Theodore Roethke.

'Admission': 'May the cat eat you & the devil eat the cat' is an Irish saying.

Acknowledgements

I extend my heartfelt gratitude to my editors, Anne Kennedy and Sue Wootton, as well as to Fiona Moffat, Meg Hamilton and everyone at Otago University Press.

Thank you also to Chris Price and the IIML MA poetry and creative nonfiction class of 2013. I am grateful to Tim Groves for allowing the use of his Film Studies lecture notes in the poem 'An analysis of us as a film', and to Adelle McNeice, Sarah Scott and Virginia Lee for their insightful feedback on the manuscript.

Special thanks to my friends Barbara, Katy, Jo, Ramola, Sarah, Spomenka and Zayna; my Arapaki friends; Debbie Newlove, Cil Van den Brink and Teresa Booth; and Virginia for her enduring friendship and for suggesting a cyanotype for the cover.

Finally, I want to thank my family – Jim, Sue, Adelle, Gareth, Beau, James, Wendy, Ben and Adam.

I also acknowledge the editors of *JAAM*, *Mayhem*, *Sport*, *Takahe* and *Turbine|Kapohau*, where versions of some of these poems were previously published.

Published by Otago University Press
Te Whare Tā o Ōtākou Whakaihu Waka
533 Castle Street
Dunedin, New Zealand
university.press@otago.ac.nz
oup.nz

First published 2024
Copyright © Jo McNeice
The moral rights of the author have been asserted.

ISBN 978-1-99-004882-1

A catalogue record for this book is available from the National Library
of New Zealand. This book is copyright. Except for the purpose of fair
review, no part may be stored or transmitted in any form or by any means,
electronic or mechanical, including recording or storage in any information
retrieval system, without permission in writing from the publishers.
No reproduction may be made, whether by photocopying or by any other
means, unless a licence has been obtained from the publisher.

Published with the assistance of Creative New Zealand

Editors: Anne Kennedy, Sue Wootton
Design/layout: Fiona Moffat
Cover: Annemarie Hope-Cross

Printed in New Zealand by Ligare